Tigers

By Patricia Janes

Children's Press®

An Imprint of Scholastic Inc.

Content Consultant
Adam Felts
Curator, Asia Quest and Heart of Africa
Columbus Zoo and Aquarium

Library of Congress Cataloging-in-Publication Data
Names: Janes, Patricia, author.
Title: Tigers/by Patricia Janes.
Other titles: Nature's children (New York, N.Y.)
Description: New York, NY: Children's Press, an imprint of Scholastic Inc., 2018. |
Series: Nature's children | Includes index.
Identifiers: LCCN 2017032753| ISBN 9780531234778 (library binding) | ISBN 9780531245071 (pbk.)
Subjects: LCSH: Tiger—Juvenile literature. | Endangered species—Juvenile literature.
Classification: LCC QL737.C23 J3635 2018 | DDC 599.756—dc23
LC record available at https://lccn.loc.gov/2017032753

Design by Anna Tunick Tabachnik

Creative Direction: Judith Christ-Lafond for Scholastic

Produced by Spooky Cheetah Press

Printed in China 62

SCHOLASTIC, CHILDREN'S PRESS, NATURE'S CHILDREN™, and associated logos
are trademarks and/or registered trademarks of Scholastic Inc.

2 3 4 5 6 7 8 9 10 R 27 26 25 24 23 22 21 20 19 18

Scholastic Inc., 557 Broadway, New York, NY 10012.

Photos ©: cover: Frank Pali/Getty Images; 1: Kantapatp/Getty Images; 4 leaf silo and throughout: stockgraphicdesigns.com;
5 tiger silo: Ellika/Shutterstock; 5 child silo: All-Silhouettes.com; 5 bottom: Zoran Kolundzija/iStockphoto; 6 tiger icon and
throughout: Airin.dizain/Shutterstock; 7: Jason Edwards/Getty Images; 8-9: Steve Winter/Getty Images; 10: Tatami_Skanks/
iStockphoto; 11: Kantapatp/Getty Images; 12-13: E.a. Kuttapan/NPL/Minden Pictures; 15: Steve Winter/Getty Images; 16-17: Andy
Rouse/Nature Picture Library; 19 top right: MHGALLERY/iStockphoto; 19 bottom left: Pete Oxford/Minden Pictures;
19 bottom right: STRDEL/AFP/Getty Images; 19 top left: Victoryakht/Dreamstime; 21: MiStock/Getty Images; 22-23: Justin
Sullivan/Getty Images; 24-25: Todd Ryburn Photography/Getty Images; 26: Mike Hill/Getty Images; 29: Gary Takeuchi;
30-31: Don Johnston/Getty Images; 33: Malcolm MacGregor/Getty Images; 35: Andy Rouse/Nature Picture Library; 36-37:
BAY ISMOYO/AFP/Getty Images; 38-39: Minden Pictures; 40-41: Yuri Smityuk/TASS/Getty Images; 42 top left: lightstock/
iStockphoto; 42 bottom left: Anan Kaewkhammul/Shutterstock; 42 right: GlobalP/iStockphoto; 43 bottom: Paul Chesley/Getty
Images; 43 top: Dennis W Donohue/Shutterstock.

Maps by Jim McMahon.

Table of Contents

Fact File: Tigers

World Distribution
China, India, Indonesia (Sumatra), Nepal, Southeast Asia (Laos, Malaysia, Myanmar, and Thailand), Russia

Russia

Nepal

China

Southeast Asia

India

Indonesia

Population Status
All subspecies are endangered, some critically; others are extinct

Habitats
Forests, grasslands, and swamps

Habits
Mostly active at night; use sight and hearing to hunt animals for food; communicate with scent, body language, and sounds like growls and snarls; usually live alone

Diet
Mainly large, hoofed animals like deer, pigs, cows, oxen, and elk

Distinctive Features
Light yellow-orange to deep reddish-orange fur with dark stripes; large padded feet for stalking prey; long claws and canine teeth for catching and killing prey

Fast Fact
The sound of a tiger's roar can travel 2 mi. (3.2 km).

Average Size

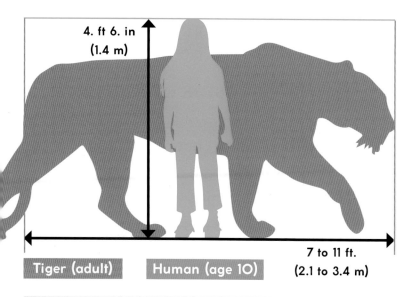

4. ft 6. in
(1.4 m)

7 to 11 ft.
(2.1 to 3.4 m)

Tiger (adult)   Human (age 10)

Taxonomy

CLASS
Mammalia (mammals)

ORDER
Carnivora
(tigers, bears, hyenas,
seals, related animals)

FAMILY
Felidae (cats)

GENUS
Panthera
(tigers, lions, leopards,
snow leopards, jaguars)

SPECIES
Panthera tigris (tigers)

LIVING SUBSPECIES
- *altaica*
  (Amur or Siberian)
- *amoyensis*
  (South China)
- *corbetti* (Indochinese)
- *jacksoni* (Malayan)
- *sumatrae* (Sumatran)
- *tigris* (Bengal)

◀ Every tiger has a
unique stripe pattern.

CHAPTER 1

Endangered Tigers

It's nighttime and the forest is quiet.

A deer drinks from a river. Nearby, a clump of tall grass moves ever so slightly, but the deer doesn't notice. Suddenly, a streak of color rushes toward the deer. With its reddish-orange fur and black stripes, the **predator** is unmistakable. It's a tiger, and it is hungry!

Tigers are a type of big cat. In fact, these meat-eaters are the largest species of cat in the world. A century ago, about 100,000 tigers prowled Asia. Today, no more than 3,900 are left in the wild.

Tigers live in small pockets of 11 countries in Asia. There were once nine different groups, or **subspecies**, of tigers. Three of these groups have died out. Only six subspecies of tigers remain. Due to overhunting, logging, and illegal trading, they are all **endangered**.

▶ The Sumatran tiger is found only on the island of Sumatra. In 2017, fewer than 400 existed.

Fast Fact
Unlike most cats,
tigers like water.
They can swim
for miles.

Home, Sweet Home

Tigers live in amazingly diverse **habitats**. They roam Asia's forests, grasslands, and swamps. These habitats may appear to have very little in common. But they all share three characteristics. They have plenty of trees or tall grasses for the tiger to take cover in. They have lots of **prey**. And they all have water to drink.

The various subspecies of tigers have developed special **adaptations** that allow them to survive in their habitats. Siberian tigers, for instance, live in the birch forests of Russia. It is cold and snowy there. These tigers have long, thick fur that keeps them warm. Sumatran tigers live in the wet rain forests of Indonesia. They have only small amounts of white fur compared with other tigers. Too much white would make them stand out as they move around in green rain forests. Bengal tigers are adapted to hot, dry regions.

◀ A Bengal tiger cub
takes a dip to cool off.

Built to Hunt

All tigers are **carnivores**. They eat meat. There are few animals better suited to hunting than the tiger. Its body is designed to kill prey.

Tigers are best known for their stripes. But they have a variety of adaptations that make them fierce predators. Tigers have large padded feet so they can move without making a sound. Whiskers on their face aid them in exploring their environment through touch as they roam in the dark. Long claws help grip prey. Two pairs of sharp **canine** teeth stab into the flesh of their victims.

Each tiger subspecies is slightly different in size. Males are typically bigger than females. Siberian tigers are the largest of these big cats. They can grow up to 10 feet (3.1 meters) long. They weigh as much as 650 pounds (294.8 kilograms). That is about the same weight as nine 10-year-old humans! The smallest subspecies is the Sumatran tiger. It may be half the weight of the Siberian tiger, but it is still huge!

Claws
are up to 4 in. (10.2 cm) long; when not in use, they are pulled into toes.

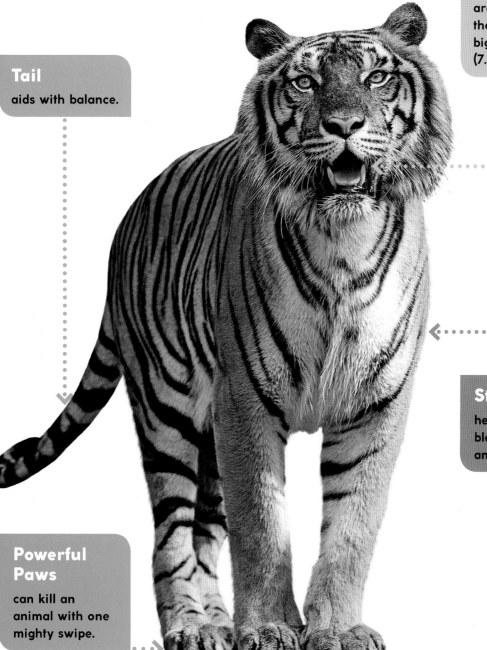

Tail
aids with balance.

Canine Teeth
are longer than those of any other big cat—up to 3 in. (7.6 cm).

Striped Coat
helps the tiger blend in with trees and grasses.

Powerful Paws
can kill an animal with one mighty swipe.

What's With Those Stripes?

Dazzling reddish-orange fur. Bold black stripes. These might not be the first colors that come to mind when you think of trying to blend in. But for tigers, the combination couldn't be better.

Most of the animals that tigers prey on don't see colors well, so a bright coat isn't a problem. And a tiger's stripes help it blend in with the grasses and trees where it lives. This **camouflage** makes the predator hard to spot. The stripes also break up the outline of the tiger's body. Animals don't notice the tiger until it's too late.

A tiger's stripes are not only on its fur. They are also on its skin! The stripes can be light brown or black. Some may be wide and others may be narrow. They can even be oval-shaped. Scientists can tell individual tigers apart by looking at their stripes.

◀ The stripes on these Bengal tigers are less dense than those of Sumatran tigers, which have the closest stripes of any subspecies.

CHAPTER 2

To Be a Tiger

Lazy days and active nights are common for tigers. They are mostly **nocturnal**. Tigers spend their nights stalking prey, feeding, or guarding a kill. On an average night, these big cats eat around 33 to 40 lb. (15 to 18.1 kg) of meat. That would be like you eating 160 quarter-pound hamburgers for dinner!

A tiger gets tired after a busy night of hunting. Daytime is a time to recharge. The tiger finds a spot that is close to water and has plenty of trees or grasses for cover. Then the cat grooms itself with its rough tongue. It licks its paws, chest, and back. Grooming keeps the tiger's coat in good shape. It removes loose hairs and dirt. After grooming, the tiger takes a nap. It will get up when nighttime approaches.

▶ Scientists used remote cameras to photograph this Indochinese tiger hunting.

Fast Fact
A tiger's night vision is about six times better than ours.

Sneak Attack

Tigers are accomplished hunters. They mainly eat large hoofed animals. Deer, wild pigs, and wild cows are all on the menu. So are oxen and elk. If food is scarce, tigers will also dine on grass, berries, and eggs.

These predators are **stealthy**. They rely on the element of surprise to kill prey. Sometimes a tiger waits quietly until an animal comes close. Then it pounces. Other times, a tiger actively tracks down prey. The big cat **navigates** by using its good hearing and night vision. It moves silently on padded feet. For now its claws are pulled into its toes. But they won't stay that way for long. The tiger creeps to within 40 ft. (12.2 m) of its prey, still being careful to stay hidden. At the very last minute, it lunges toward the animal. The tiger's claws spring out and become bladelike weapons. It sinks its long canine teeth into the animal's neck.

◀ A Bengal tiger brings down a Sambar deer in India.

Top Predator

Tigers are apex predators. That means they sit at the top of the food chain and have few natural enemies. Rarely, a dhole will attack a tiger. These Asiatic wild dogs don't usually hunt tigers, though. Attacks might happen when a tiger and a pack of dholes cross paths. Other animals may attack tigers to defend themselves.

Humans are the greatest threat to tigers. People hunt the big cats and destroy their habitats. When tigers are threatened, their whole **ecosystem** is at risk. If the tiger **population** goes down, fewer prey like deer and wild pigs get eaten. Populations of those animals rise. More deer and wild pigs then eat more plants. That leaves less food for other plant-eating animals. This ripple effect disrupts the balance of nature.

It is important that people protect tigers. By doing so, we protect the entire ecosystem.

▶ Tigers feed mostly on medium to large hoofed animals called ungulates.

Saiga Antelope

Tigers hunt this hoofed animal, which is native to Asia.

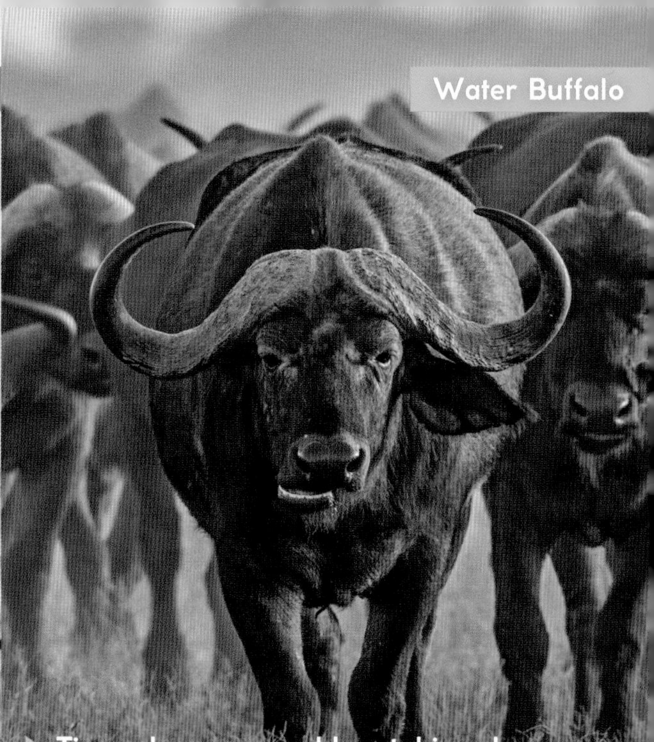

Water Buffalo

▶ Tigers have no problem taking down large prey like water buffalo.

Wild Pig

▶ Tigers are a main predator of wild boars, also known as wild pigs, in Asia.

Sambar Deer

▶ This large deer makes up as much as 60 percent of the Bengal tiger's diet.

CHAPTER 3

Growing Up Tiger

Between hunting, grooming, and crisscrossing the landscape, tigers keep busy. Females lead especially busy lives. They are tasked with caring for their young. Male tigers don't help raise cubs.

Female tigers are ready to reproduce at three or four years old. A female mates with a male tiger that lives close by. About three months later she prepares to give birth. She searches for the perfect spot to have her young. An ideal **den** is tucked away to keep her cubs safely hidden. It also has plenty of prey nearby so the mom can eat.

The female tiger gives birth to a litter of two to four cubs. Then she spends the next two years raising them. She teaches the cubs how to survive on their own. With any luck, they will live 10 to 15 years.

▶ Cubs, like this young Siberian tiger, are usually born into a litter consisting of roughly an equal number of males and females.

Under Mom's Care

Life is tough for a tiger cub. About half of all cubs do not survive more than two years. Some die of starvation or illness. Unlike full-grown tigers, cubs are vulnerable to predators. Some may even be killed by male tigers who want to mate with the cubs' mother.

Newborns are especially vulnerable. They weigh only 2 to 3 lb. (0.9 to 1.4 kg) at birth. That's about the weight of eight sticks of butter! It is important that predators don't detect the scent of cubs. If they do, they might attack. A mom licks her newborns' fur to remove their scent. She may even eat their waste. That keeps the den from getting smelly.

Like other **mammals**, newborn cubs drink milk from their mother. She will add meat to their diet when they are about six weeks old. They will stop **nursing** altogether around their first birthday.

◀ A Sumatran tiger gently carries her cub with her teeth.

23

Playtime Is Serious Business

A cub bats its mom's tail. Another does a somersault. Then it swats its sibling. This may look like just fun and games, but it's actually more like school time! These cubs are learning how to hunt and protect themselves.

A tiger must be able to stalk and pounce on prey. It must also be able to strike an enemy. Starting at about nine months old, cubs join their mom on hunts. They watch and learn her tactics. They begin to practice these moves on their siblings. The cubs' mother also allows them to kill prey that she has already injured.

By the time the cubs are one and a half years old, they start hunting on their own. They also begin to explore more. The cubs will go farther and farther from the safety of their den. At around age two, it's time for these **solitary** animals to leave home.

▶ In most litters, there is a dominant cub—usually a male—that consumes more resources and takes the lead at playtime.

24

Stay off My Turf!

Siblings may stick together for a little while after leaving their mother. But the tigers will drift away from each other before long. Each will stake out its own **territory**. It is there that the tiger will live and hunt.

Males have larger territories than females do. The size depends on how much prey is available. In places that are teeming with prey, a territory may be as small as 2 to 60 square miles (5.2 to 155.4 square kilometers). Walt Disney World, which is 40 sq. mi. (103.6 sq. km), could fit inside a territory on the larger end. In other places, prey is harder to find. When that's the case, territories can be 300 to 450 sq. mi. (777 to 1,165.5 sq. km). That's equal to or bigger than New York City.

A tiger is protective of its territory. The cat marks it as its own. It does so by leaving behind urine or droppings. It also scratches trees. These markings tell other tigers, "Stay away!"

◀ Adult cats, like these Siberian tigers, risk injury or even death when they fight to defend their territory.

CHAPTER 4

An Ancient History

Scientists study fossils to learn how species are related. They have discovered a lot about how tigers **evolved** from ancient animals.

Cats belong to the family known as Felidae. All members of the Felidae family share an early **ancestor**. This common ancestor, called *Pseudaelurus*, likely lived in central Asia 10.8 million years ago. Over time the cats began to differ from one another. Now there are four main groups of cats. One group is the big cats. Scientists call this group *Panthera*. It includes tigers, lions, jaguars, leopards, and snow leopards. Another group is the small cats. This group includes all of the smaller wild cats, as well as domestic cats. The remaining two groups are cheetahs and clouded leopards.

▶ Scientists have found fossils of the now-extinct *Panthera blytheae* in the Himalayan mountains of Asia. It is the oldest known big cat.

Family Ties

For decades, scientists had been trying to piece together the exact relationships between the different groups of big cats. Finally, in 2010, scientists got some clues. A group of researchers studied **DNA** from each of the five species of big cats. They concluded that lions, leopards, and jaguars are more closely related to each other than they are to tigers and snow leopards. These three species share a common ancestor. That ancestor split from other cats between 4.3 million and 3.8 million years ago.

Tigers seem to be most closely related to snow leopards. Tigers and snow leopards also share a common ancestor. It lived about 3.9 million years ago. The tiger began to evolve into a unique species about 3.2 million years ago. The tiger and snow leopard are both among the most endangered of the big cats.

◀ Snow leopards live in the high, rugged mountains of central Asia. Large paws help keep them from sinking into snow.

31

Tiger vs. Kitty

House cats love to swat at fake mice. And if there's more than one cat in a household, they'll often wrestle. House cats look and act a lot like tigers—and for good reason. They are relatives. Tigers and domestic cats share about 95.6 percent of their DNA. So they have a lot in common.

Although their human owners may serve them kibble, domestic cats are carnivores just like tigers. Both species are built to stalk, leap, and pounce on prey. Domestic cats are naturally skilled at hunting birds and small rodents. They are also nocturnal. House cats sleep a lot during the day and are active at night. The same is true for tigers.

One interesting difference? Tigers can roar. So can most of the other big cats. But house cats can't. Scientists believe that's because of differences in the two cats' throats. Those differences also explain why house cats can purr but tigers don't seem to be able to. Instead, tigers chuff to greet each other.

▶ Domestic cats that have stripes are called tabby cats.

A Future at Risk

Tigers are one of the most recognized animals on Earth. Yet their future looks grim. These big cats once roamed much of Asia. Now they are gone from 96 percent of their historic range. Three out of nine subspecies are **extinct**. Another, the South China tiger, is thought to be extinct in the wild. No one has seen signs of that big cat in its natural habitat in more than 10 years. Only the Bengal, Indochinese, Sumatran, Siberian, and Malayan subspecies remain. Scientists have declared Sumatran and Malayan tigers critically endangered. That means there's an extremely high risk that these subspecies will die out in the wild.

Conservation efforts are giving tigers a fighting chance. For 100 years, tiger populations had been on the decline. Finally their numbers are rising. But more needs to be done if tigers are to survive.

▶ People can visit parks in India to see Bengal tigers like this one.

Threats at Every Turn

Tigers face many threats. Some people keep tigers as pets or in roadside attractions. Conservation scientists estimate that there may be between 5,000 and 10,000 captive tigers in the United States. That's about twice the number of wild tigers in Asia!

People also overhunt the animals that tigers prey on, like deer, elk, and wild pigs. This leaves the big cats with little food to eat. To make matters worse, suitable tiger habitat is shrinking. People are clearing land to make way for buildings. They are turning forests into farms. This is called deforestation. A tiger's territory may shrink or overlap with that of other tigers. Then the tigers have to compete with one another for resources.

When tigers can't find enough food, they may attack people's livestock. It's the only way the big cats can survive and feed their cubs. In response to these attacks, people may kill the tigers. They do this to protect their livestock, families, and communities.

◀ Forests in Indonesia have been cleared to make way for palm oil plantations.

Killed for Parts

The biggest danger to tigers is **poaching**. It is illegal to hunt tigers, but people do it anyway. They sell tiger body parts as food, for souvenirs, or for use in traditional medicines. Some people believe medicines made with tiger parts can treat illnesses or injuries.

For example, people in China have long used tiger parts in medicine. Each part of the tiger has a different use. It is said that a cream made out of a tiger's tail cures skin disorders. The blood is believed to give a person strength. The big cat's whiskers are made into a medicine to cure toothaches. Scientists have proven that there is no medical benefit to any of these so-called traditional cures.

These practices are more than 3,000 years old. Today, most people who practice ancient Chinese medicine no longer use tiger parts. They realize that killing the animals for medicines endangers the species.

▶ These packets of traditional medicines are made from tiger bones.

Holding Out Hope

Scientists all around the world, from universities to zoos, work to protect tigers. They teach the public about the dangers tigers face. They hope people will think twice before they kill a tiger or destroy its habitat.

Conservation scientists also help save tigers that are hurt or have been **abandoned** by their mothers. One day in 2015, an abandoned Siberian tiger cub walked into a village in Russia. It was starving. It was looking for food. Poachers had likely killed its mother. Villagers named the cub Filippa. They brought her to a **rehabilitation** center. Veterinarians cared for Filippa until she was healthy again. They taught her how to hunt and survive on her own. They cared for her for about two years. Then Filippa was strong enough to return to the wild. Conservation scientists released her into a forest in Russia.

Scientists think efforts like these may save tigers from extinction. They hope everyone will do their part to protect these amazing cats.

◄ This tiger was released back into the wilds of Russia in 2016.

Tiger Family Tree

Tigers belong to the genus *Panthera*, also known as big cats. All the animals in this genus are carnivores and sit at the top of the food chain. They all have a common ancestor that lived about 6 million years ago. This diagram shows how tigers are related to other big cats, such as leopards, jaguars, lions, and snow leopards. The closer together two animals are on the tree, the more similar they are.

Leopards
**spotted big cats
that often stalk
prey from trees**

Jaguars
**the largest of
South America's
big cats**

**Ancestor
of all
Big Cats**

Note: Animal photos are not to scale.

Lions
big cats that
usually live in
groups
called prides

Snow Leopards
big cats known for
their smoky-gray
fur coat with dark
gray spots

Tigers
the largest cat
species; known for
its dark stripes and
reddish fur coat

Words to Know

A .... **abandoned** *(uh-BAN-duhnd)* deserted or no longer being cared for

adaptations *(ad-ap-TAY-shuns)* changes a living thing goes through so it fits in better within its environment

ancestor *(ANN-ses-tur)* a family member who lived long ago

C .... **camouflage** *(KAM-uh-flahzh)* a disguise or a natural coloring that allows animals, people, or objects to hide by making them look like their surroundings

canine *(KAY-nine)* one of the pointed teeth on each side of the upper and lower jaws

captive *(KAP-tiv)* living in the care of people

carnivores *(KAHR-nuh-vorz)* animals that eat meat

D .... **den** *(DEN)* the home of a wild animal

DNA *(DEE-en-AY)* the molecule that carries our genes, found inside the nucleus of cells

E .... **ecosystem** *(EE-koh-sis-tuhm)* all the living things in a place and their relation to their environment

endangered *(en-DAYN-juhrd)* a plant or animal that is in danger of becoming extinct, usually because of human activity

evolved *(i-VAHLVD)* changed slowly and naturally over time

extinct *(ik-STINGKT)* no longer found alive

F .... **fossils** *(FAH-suhls)* bones, shells, or other traces of animals or plants from millions of years ago, preserved as rock

H .... **habitats** *(HAB-i-tats)* the places where an animal or plant is usually found

M .... **mammals** *(MAM-uhlz)* warm-blooded animals that have hair or fur and usually give birth to live babies; female mammals produce milk to feed their young

N .... **navigates** *(NAV-i-gates)* finds which way to go

nocturnal *(nahk-TUR-nuhl)* active at night

nursing *(NURS-ing)* drinking milk from a breast

P .... **poaching** *(POHCH-ing)* hunting or fishing illegally on someone else's property

population *(pahp-yuh-LAY-shuhn)* all members of a species living in a certain place

predator *(PRED-uh-tuhr)* an animal that lives by hunting other animals for food

prey *(PRAY)* an animal that is hunted by another animal for food

R .... **rehabilitation** *(ree-huh-bill-ih-TAY-shun)* the process of bringing an animal back to health

S .... **solitary** *(SAH-li-ter-ee)* not requiring or without the companionship of others

stealthy *(STEL-thee)* acting with silence, secrecy, and caution

subspecies *(sub-SPEE-sheez)* a group of related plants or animals that is smaller than a species; a division of a species

T .... **territory** *(TER-i-tor-ee)* an area that an animal or group of animals uses and defends

Find Out More

BOOKS

- Clutton-Brock, Juliet. *DK Eyewitness Books: Cat*. New York: DK Publishing, 2014.
- Marsico, Katie. *Big Cats* (A True Book). New York: Scholastic Inc., 2017.
- Simon, Seymour. *Big Cats*. New York: Harper Collins, 2017.

WEB PAGES

- www.worldwildlife.org/species/tiger

  Read about the various tiger subspecies and how people are helping these at-risk animals.

- www.panthera.org/cat/tiger

  Panthera is the only organization in the world devoted to the conservation of wild cats, including big cats, cheetahs, and pumas.

- www.seaworld.org/en/animal-info/animal-infobooks/tiger

  Learn more about the behavior of tigers, as well as the risks they face and what's being done to protect them.

Facts for Now

Visit this Scholastic Web site for more information on tigers:
www.factsfornow.scholastic.com Enter the keyword Tigers

Index

Index (continued)

About the Author

Patricia Janes has nearly two decades of experience writing about science for children. She had three cats growing up, so she was excited to learn all about their wild relative—the tiger. Now she has a dog, Henry, and lives in Westchester, NY, with her husband and son.

THE EAR
AND HEARING

The Human Body

THE EAR
AND HEARING

Brian R. Ward

Series consultant:
Dr. A. R. Maryon-Davis
MB, BChir, MSc, MRCS, MRCP

The Human Body

Franklin Watts
London New York Sydney Toronto

First published in Great Britain 1981 by
Franklin Watts Limited
12a Golden Square
London W1

First published in the United States of America by
Franklin Watts Inc.
387 Park Avenue South
New York, N.Y. 10016

UK ISBN: 0 85166 930 1
US ISBN: 0-531-04289-8
Library of Congress Catalog Card No: 80-54826

Designed by Howard Dyke

Acknowledgments

The illustrations were prepared by: Andrew Aloof,
Marion Appleton, Nick Cudworth, The Diagram Group,
Howard Dyke, David Holmes, David Mallott.

Contents

Introduction

The ear is much more complicated than it might appear at first. The external ears, on each side of the head, are merely sound collectors, while the real work is done by a very delicate and involved mechanism buried deep within the bones of the skull.

Our hearing is very sensitive (although many animals hear better), but it often becomes weaker with age, as do most of our other senses. This may be partly a result of the noisy society in which we live. People who have always lived in quiet country areas can often hear well right into old age, while even young people living in noisy towns have some loss in their hearing ability. Very young babies have extremely acute hearing, and are often startled by small sounds which would scarcely be noticed by an older child or an adult.

A deaf person can move about freely and lead a relatively normal life, but if some of the other parts of the ear are damaged, it would be very difficult even to walk. As well as being an organ of hearing, the inner ear is an organ of balance, allowing us to make all the tiny corrections in muscle movement which enable us to move about confidently and without clumsiness. It also contains special organs which tell us how the head is positioned, making it easy for us to keep our balance and walk steadily even in total darkness, when our position cannot be measured by the eyes.

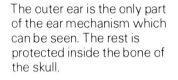

The outer ear is the only part of the ear mechanism which can be seen. The rest is protected inside the bone of the skull.

The parts of the ear

The ear is divided into three separate parts, each with its own special functions.

The **outer ear** consists of the visible ear, a tube about 1 in (2.5 cm) long and the **eardrum**, or **tympanic membrane**.

Just behind the eardrum, in a small, hollow area in the skull, is the **middle ear**, which contains three tiny bones. The middle ear acts as a simple mechanical amplifier which increases the strength of sounds entering the ear. It is filled with air, and

The ear mechanism is divided into three separate areas. The outer ear is visible at the side of the head, but the middle and inner ear are protected within the skull.

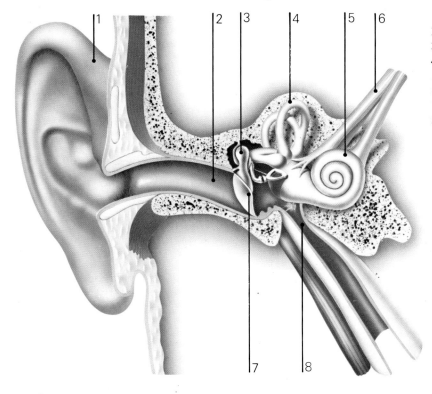

1 outer ear
2 ear canal
3 auditory ossicles
4 semicircular canals
5 cochlea
6 auditory nerve
7 eardrum
8 eustachian tube

8

sound is carried along the three bones it contains.

The most complicated part is the **inner ear**, where the sense organs for both hearing and balance are situated. The inner ear is a delicate, hollow structure, made of very thin tissue. It fits snugly into a space in the bone of the skull called the **bony labyrinth**, which supports the delicate tubes called the **membranous labyrinth**. The **cochlea** is the part of the inner ear concerned with hearing. It is a tightly coiled tube, wound in a spiral with $2\frac{3}{4}$ turns.

Three looped tubes called **semicircular canals** detect the movement of the head in any direction. At the base of each canal, is a bulge called the **ampulla** containing the actual sense organs of balance.

At the point where the three canals come together is another bulge called the **utricle**. Nearby is another balloon-like swelling called the **saccule**. Both of these structures are concerned with detecting changes in position of the head.

Unlike the middle ear, the whole membranous labyrinth of the inner ear is filled with liquid, which is necessary to maintain its shape, and to carry sound to the parts where sensory cells are positioned.

Understanding sound

Sound is a form of energy, as are electricity and light. All forms of energy can travel long distances, and electricity and light travel almost instantaneously. Compared to these, sound travels very slowly, as you will notice when you see a bat strike a ball, and then hear the sound a moment later. When lightning strikes, you may not hear the sound for several seconds.

Modern jetliners now travel at a speed which is very close to the speed of sound. The speed of modern aircraft is now measured against the speed of sound, called Mach 1; the speed of the aircraft is then described as Mach 1.5, Mach 2 and so on. The speed of sound is about 760 mph (1,220 km/h), but becomes lower as a plane flies higher. This is because sound travels faster in more solid materials and more slowly in the thin air at high altitudes. It travels 20,000 times as fast through steel as through air; four times as fast through water.

Sound travels in waves. When a sound is produced, it causes the tiny molecules in the air (or in any other material) to vibrate back and forth, striking the molecules next to them. This, in turn, starts the next molecules vibrating, and the sound is carried along like a row of dominoes being knocked over.

Sound is produced by the rapidly vibrating arms of a tuning fork. Although the movement is too fast to be seen, it can be made visible by dipping the vibrating tuning fork into water.

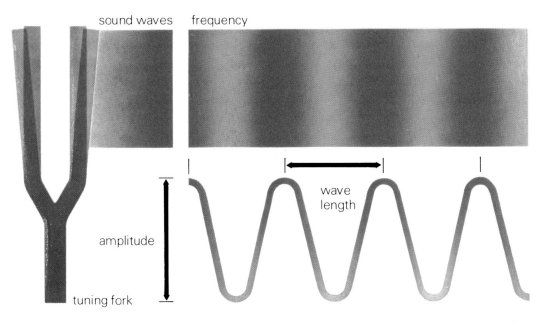

sound waves   frequency

wave
length

amplitude

tuning fork

Molecules vibrate from side to side, as well as back and forth. They produce widening areas of disturbance in nearby molecules, and the disturbance is carried along in a continuing up-and-down movement, like a series of "S" shapes joined end to end. This is called a **sound wave**. Each molecule soon returns to its original position, so only its energy is passed along.

The shape of a sound wave is very important, as it governs the actual sounds we hear. The *height* of the wave, measured as hills or valleys, is the amount that molecules move up or down, and is important in governing the *volume*, or loudness, of sound we hear. The *distance between* the hills or valleys is called the **wave length. Frequency** is the number of back-and-forth movements the molecules make each second, or cycles per second, and this governs how shrill or deep the sound seems.

The vibrating arms of a tuning fork generate sound waves, as they cause the molecules in the air to move back and forth and up and down. The air is alternately compressed and rarified with each vibrating movement of the arms of the tuning fork.

11

The limits of hearing

The "voices" of animals and man vary very widely in the pitch of the sound they produce, measured in cycles per second. Bats can produce only very shrill, high-frequency sounds, while our own voices are lower, but can produce a wide range of notes.
The sounds heard by man and by other animals are often quite different from those they produce.

The human ear is not only very sensitive, but is also discriminating. This means that we can detect minute differences in the sounds we hear, which is how we can understand the spoken word, and appreciate music.

Our speaking voices usually range between 100 and 150 cycles per second (c/s, or hertz, the more modern description). The highest sounds are about 20,000 c/s, a high-pitched hiss, while the lowest is 10 c/s, when we literally *feel* the sound as a low rumble.

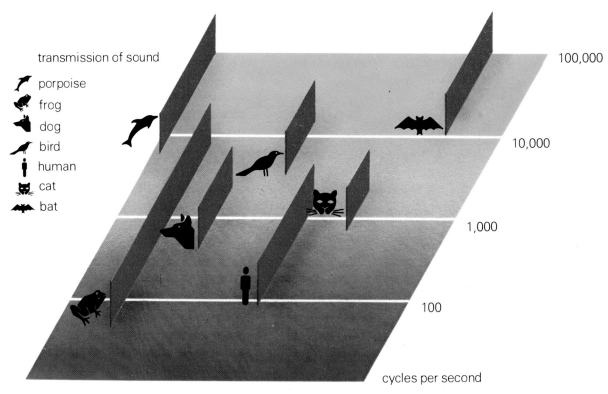

transmission of sound

porpoise
frog
dog
bird
human
cat
bat

100,000

10,000

1,000

100

cycles per second

Between these upper and lower limits, we can distinguish more than 1,500 different frequencies.

Loudness is measured in units called bels, named after Alexander Graham Bell, inventor of the telephone. The quietest sound we can hear is 0 bels, while a quiet whisper is about 30 **decibels** (a decibel is one-tenth of a bel). Normal conversation is 60 decibels, while noises of 120 decibels, like a jet aircraft taking off, can actually be painful.

Dogs have extremely sensitive hearing, and can hear sounds which are too high pitched for us to detect. A "supersonic" dog whistle produces this high-frequency sound, which cannot usually be heard by the human ear.

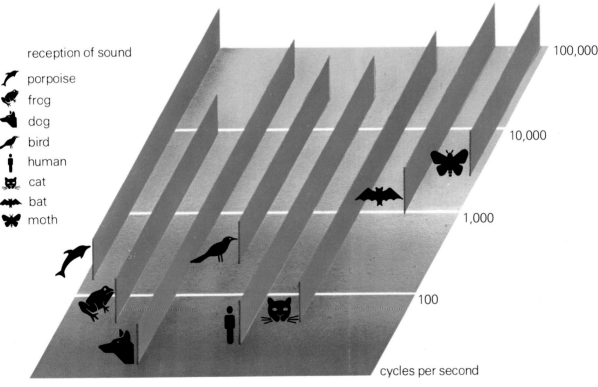

reception of sound

porpoise
frog
dog
bird
human
cat
bat
moth

100,000

10,000

1,000

100

cycles per second

13

The outer ear

The outer ear acts as a funnel, conveying sound waves along the ear canal so that they strike the eardrum, and cause it to vibrate. The eardrum, or tympanic membrane, is a thin but tough structure which, when vibrated by sound waves entering the ear, transfers the movement to the bones of the middle ear, by way of the malleus.

The visible part of the ear is called the **pinna**, or **auricle**. It is a flap made mostly from a rubbery material called cartilage. Its shape is intended to collect sounds and funnel them into the **ear canal**. The human pinna is fixed in position, but in many animals the ears can be turned like radar scanners to measure the direction from which sounds are heard. We attempt to identify direction by turning our heads until the sounds are heard equally strongly by each ear, when we face directly

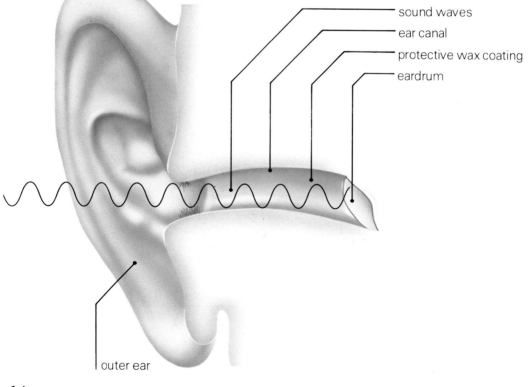

sound waves

ear canal

protective wax coating

eardrum

outer ear

toward the sound. This is less accurate than an animal's movable ears, but even so, we can detect the direction from which a sound is coming to within three degrees.

Sound is directed by the pinna into the ear canal, at the end of which is the eardrum, or tympanic membrane. The short ear canal is lined with very thin skin, covered in fine hairs. In the lining are tiny glands which secrete sticky **cerumen**, or wax. This helps to trap dust which would otherwise settle on the eardrum.

The eardrum is a thin, heart-shaped membrane stretched across the end of the ear canal, over an opening leading into the middle ear. It contains criss-crossed fibers which make it quite strong, although it can be punctured if sharp objects are poked into the ear. Attached to its middle is the end of one of the tiny bones of the middle ear, called the **malleus**, or hammer.

Sound waves, directed down the ear canal by the pinna, strike the eardrum. Energy from the sound waves is transferred to the eardrum, causing it to vibrate strongly. This is the first part of the process of hearing.

The human ear is adapted to hear a wide range of sounds, although our hearing is less sensitive than that of many animals. The rabbit needs sensitive hearing for protection against other animals, hence its large movable ears. Birds depend more on sight than hearing, and their slit-like ears are hidden beneath their feathers.

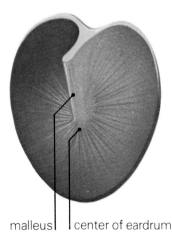

malleus | center of eardrum

The middle ear

The middle ear acts as an amplifier, stepping up the vibrations of the eardrum, and passing them on to the inner ear, where the sense organs are situated.

Vibrations are conducted through three very small bones. The first of these, the malleus, is attached to the eardrum, and is moved as the eardrum vibrates.

The malleus moves against the **incus**, or anvil bone, which is suspended by fine threads of ligament so that it can move very freely in the middle-ear cavity. It is suspended and hinged in such a way that the small movements of the malleus are increased by 50 per cent at the far end of the incus.

The incus is joined, in turn, to the smallest of the three bones, the **stapes**, or stirrup. This bone is attached to another membrane called the oval window, opening into the inner ear. Vibrations are passed from the eardrum, through the three bones, and out through the oval window.

The middle ear contains important safety measures to protect the vulnerable mechanism. It is air-filled; changes in pressure, such as we experience when going up or down a high hill, cause the air to expand and contract. This pressure could force the delicate eardrum, causing damage

The complicated structure of the ear can be simplified by drawing it as a mechanical device. The diagram shows how sound is transferred by a series of levers to the fluid-filled inner ear, where it produces a nerve impulse.

drum membrane

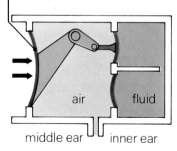

air   fluid

middle ear   inner ear

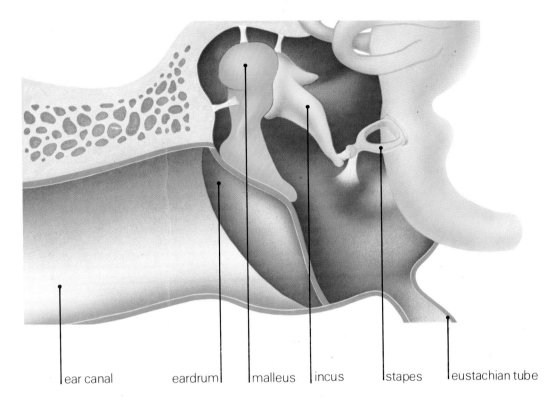

ear canal   eardrum   malleus   incus   stapes   eustachian tube

or even bursting it. But there is a long tube, the **eustachian tube**, which is connected to the throat at the back of the mouth and allows the pressure in the middle ear to be equalized with the pressure of the outside air. Air moving along this tube causes the popping we hear in the ear when ascending or descending in an aircraft.

The other safety device in the middle ear protects the mechanism from noise. When the ear is exposed to a very loud noise, tiny muscles tighten the eardrum, preventing it from moving too far as it vibrates. Another tiny muscle pulls the stapes bone away from its connection with the incus, cutting down the amount of vibration passed on to the oval window.

The middle ear acts as an amplifier, increasing vibrations caused by sounds entering the ear and passing them on to the inner ear. Its three tiny bones, or ossicles, are hinged so that they work as a series of levers.

The inner ear

In the inner ear, the mechanical movements of the eardrum and the bones of the middle ear are converted into a different form of energy, which can be carried along nerves to the brain.

The cochlea is the organ responsible for picking up these vibrations. It is part of the membranous labyrinth, a tapering, coiled spiral with a wider base, shaped like a snail shell.

It is easiest to understand the structure of the cochlea if you imagine it straightened out from its original spiral. You would then have a long tapered tube, very thin and delicate, with a bulge at the thicker end.

The cochlea is coiled like a snail's shell. Imagine it straightened out, and its structure can be seen more clearly. It contains three separate liquid-filled ducts, separated by thin membranes.

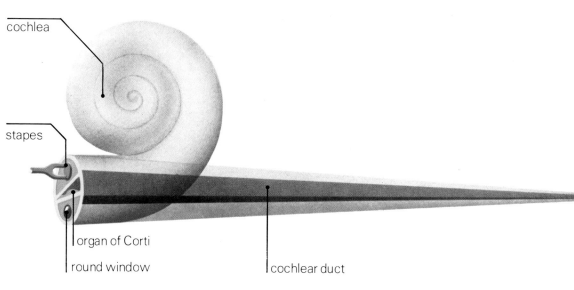

cochlea

stapes

organ of Corti

round window

cochlear duct

18

Running through the length of the cochlea are three compartments, like three tubes pressed tightly together, side by side. The oval window opens into the top tube, at its bulbous base. The bottom tube also opens on the middle ear, through a much smaller membrane-covered opening called the round window. Both the upper and lower tubes are filled with a thin liquid called **perilymph**.

The much smaller middle tube, called the cochlear duct, is also fluid-filled, and contains a different liquid called **endolymph**. The cochlear duct contains special cells which register sound vibrations and turn them into nervous signals which pass to the brain. This takes place in the **organ of Corti**, which is a strip running the whole length of the cochlea. It consists of a ribbon of very thin material, called the **tectorial membrane**, which is attached to the lining of the duct. Below this ribbon are a mass of sensory cells, each carrying a hair which is in contact with the membrane. Running from each sensory cell is a fine hair-like nerve fiber, along which a signal can be carried. The sensory cells rest on the **basilar membrane** at the bottom of the duct.

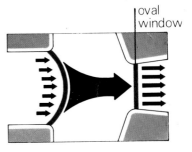

oval window

Sound is a form of energy. All the sound energy striking the eardrum is passed to the much smaller oval window. Its effects on the smaller membrane are to produce much stronger back-and-forth-movements which are in turn passed on to the cochlea.

Recording sound

A cross-section of part of the cochlea shows the sense organ called the organ of Corti. Membranes above and below the organ are moved by sound vibrations in the fluid filling the ducts. This stimulates the sense organs to produce nerve impulses.

In the inner ear, sound travels through a liquid in the form of vibrations. The sound enters the cochlea through the oval window, vibrated by the stapes bone. The sound waves travel along the upper tube, toward the tapered far end. They are able to vibrate the thin walls separating the three tubes that

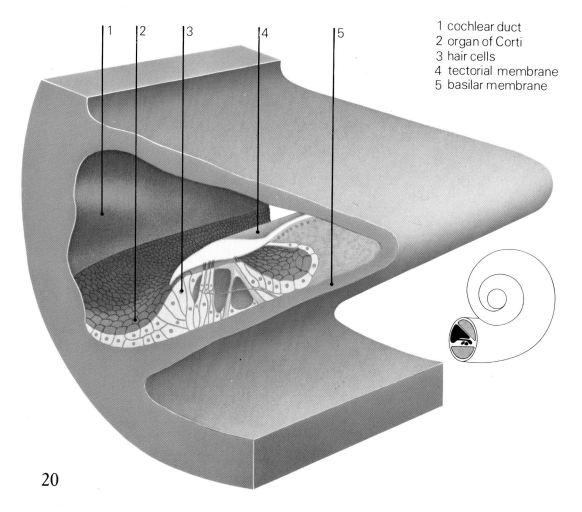

1 cochlear duct
2 organ of Corti
3 hair cells
4 tectorial membrane
5 basilar membrane

make up the cochlea, first passing the waves through the walls of the central cochlear duct, then into the lower tube. Here the waves move back toward the wider end of the cochlea, eventually losing their energy through the round window, which vibrates in the opposite direction to the oval window. Having done their job, the sound waves then pass into the air space of the middle ear.

As the sound waves pass through the side of the cochlear duct, they move the basilar membrane below the organ of Corti, so that it slides slightly against the tectorial membrane above it. This causes the hairs on the sensory cells to bend, and stimulates the cells to produce an electrical signal.

Because of the special wave shape of vibrations passing along the tapered cochlea, certain different types of stimulation of the nerve cells take place. Loud noises cause greater up-and-down movement of the waves. These, in turn, cause greater movement of the basilar membrane. Greater numbers of sensory cells are stimulated, so the brain will know that a loud noise has been recorded.

Sound waves travel for differing distances along the cochlea, depending on the frequency. This allows the ear to distinguish between sounds of different frequencies.

How sound reaches the brain

Information received in the cochlea leaves the ear as a confused mass of coded electrical signals. There are 23,000 receptor cells in the organ of Corti, and each can produce a signal. From each sensory cell runs a fine nerve fiber. These gradually bunch together to form a nerve.

Signals are passed along this **auditory nerve** to the brain. The nerve is a thick bundle of about 30,000 nerve fibers (it contains this larger number because it also carries messages from the organs of balance).

The messages carried along the nerve fibers are each very simple. The sensory cells produce a continuous, regular stream of tiny electrical signals. When they are stimulated, as their sensory hairs are bent by movements of the membrane covering them, their signals are produced much more rapidly. Bursts of extra signals are generated from the sensory cells as sounds are received. These bursts of signals pass along the nerve fibers toward the brain.

The nerve fiber passes messages very quickly, but not fast enough to allow all the signals to reach the brain directly. A sensory cell produces up to 20,000 signals each second, but a nerve fiber can transmit only 1,000 signals each second. The problem is

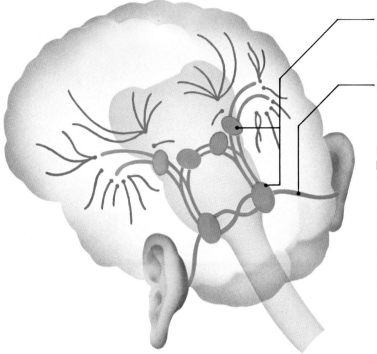

ganglia, where sounds are sorted, clarified and rerouted

auditory nerve

Nerve impulses entering the brain from the ear pass through a very complicated route, where information is exchanged with that received from the other side of the brain. At several points the nerve impulses are filtered and "cleaned up" to remove unwanted noise.

partly overcome by passing signals along different nerve fibers in turn, so more can reach the brain. But still a large number are lost or filtered out. This has the effect of reducing "noise," those random signals which are not necessary to our sense of hearing. The signal is simplified and "cleaned up."

The auditory nerve is very short, and carries sound into the base of the brain, close to the ear. Once within the brain, impulses follow an immensely complicated course to different parts of the brain. During their travels, some impulses cross to the opposite side of the brain. This probably allows sounds received from each ear to be compared, so we can decide from which direction the sound is coming.

Hearing and the brain

Every minute of the day, millions of tiny electrical signals arrive on the surface of the brain, carried by complicated pathways from the ears. They finish up on small areas on either side of the brain, called the auditory **cortex**. We know they arrive here because, if a fine wire is touched on the brain's surface in these areas, and a loud sound is produced near the ear, an electrical current will be picked up and carried through the wire, and can be used to produce a sound from a loudspeaker.

Nerve impulses traveling through the brain produce tiny electrical currents which can be measured on the brain surface. In this way, the different parts of the brain used in hearing can be identified.

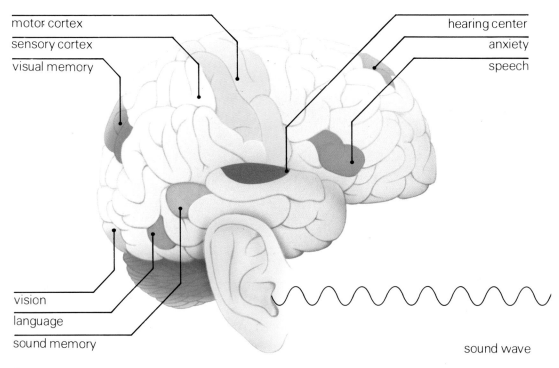

motor cortex

sensory cortex

visual memory

hearing center

anxiety

speech

vision

language

sound memory

sound wave

No one really understands how the brain uses all these signals to reproduce the sounds we hear. What is known is that the coded signals are compared with memories stored in the brain. These memories start to accumulate from the moment we are born and are built up to form a library of experiences against which signals received from the ear are checked. We can recognize about 500,000 different sounds by the time we are adults. New sounds are simply sorted out and compared with sounds in the memory. They are checked to see if they require any action or response, and then are either filed in the memory or ignored. Possibly the reason that certain discordant sounds are so disturbing, such as a fingernail scraped on a blackboard, is that these unusual sounds do not fit comfortably into our memory.

The fact remains that, although the mechanism of the ear is very well understood, the working of the brain is still largely a mystery. Scientists cannot yet say why some skilled musicians can identify a single note with perfect accuracy, while other people are tone deaf and are completely unable to sing or hum music, or recognize an ear-splitting mistake when music is played to them.

Making sense of sound

To make proper use of the flood of sounds entering the ear, we have to filter out unwanted noise. This is done at various points in the brain, where certain types of sound can be temporarily blocked off from our awareness. Every day, we have conversations with people in conditions where the background noise is much louder than the voice of the person we are talking to. Yet we can usually ignore background noise and hear the voices clearly.

Even more complicated is the ability to pick out one person's voice in a room full of chattering people. No machine can even approach the brain's ability to decipher understandable conversation from chaotic background noise.

We can even switch off almost *all* incoming sounds, if we are concentrating very hard on something. As a result we are often accused of being absent-minded or inattentive. This ability is not just due to the brain. Some regular sounds which we usually ignore, such as the ticking of a clock, are cancelled out in the ear itself, and never even reach the brain.

The ability to recognize words is almost unique to the human brain. Voice-operated typewriters have been produced, but with a limited vocabulary. They are unable to cope with all the many accents we understand as a matter of course, together with bad pronunciation and the abbreviation of words.

Sometimes we cannot distinguish very accurately between similar words, but we can identify them because of the way in which they are used. "Bark" and "park" or "bull" and "pull" sound almost identical, although we seldom confuse them in the context of a sentence.

The brain can reject unwanted sounds, so we can hear conversation clearly, even through all the normal background noise.

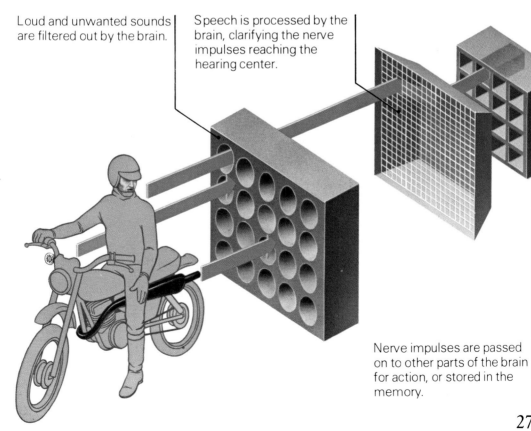

Loud and unwanted sounds are filtered out by the brain.

Speech is processed by the brain, clarifying the nerve impulses reaching the hearing center.

Nerve impulses are passed on to other parts of the brain for action, or stored in the memory.

Hearing problems

Many defects can affect our ability to hear. Everyone experiences some loss of hearing as they age, and the disability may be quite minor, or may be complete deafness.

A "normal" person can hear sounds as low as 15 decibels. A person is effectively deaf when he or she cannot hear sounds much below 80 decibels, the loudest sound produced in normal speech.

Conductive deafness is the most common type, caused when sound never actually reaches the inner ear. In its simplest form, conductive deafness can occur when the ear

Deafness or impaired hearing can be caused by anything which interferes with the entry of sound waves to the ear, their transmission to the inner ear, or by a fault in the sensory mechanism in the cochlea.

Some common causes of deafness:

1 foreign body
2 wax
3 inflammation of middle ear
4 blocked eustachian tube
5 inflammation of inner ear
6 otosclerosis

other causes:
● damage due to prolonged exposure to noise
● inherited defect at birth
● acute damage due to extremely loud noise

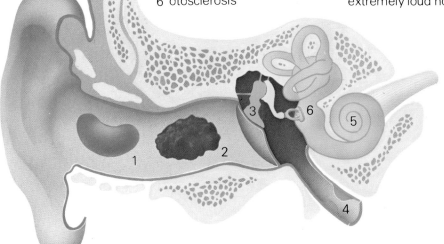

canal is blocked by wax. It is quite common in old people, and is cured by having the ears syringed by a doctor.

Temporary deafness is sometimes caused by infection of the middle ear, when inflammation prevents the movement of the middle-ear bones. If not treated, this could cause total and permanent deafness.

The most common form of conductive deafness is otosclerosis, which affects millions of people. It is caused by bony deposits which lock the stapes bone in position, and prevent it from passing vibrations on through the oval window.

Most people with conductive deafness have to rely on a hearing aid – a miniature microphone, amplifier, and loudspeaker – which picks up sound and plays it back directly into the ear, but much louder. Unfortunately, it also distorts some sounds, so speech may not be entirely clear.

The other common type of hearing problem is perceptive deafness, where there is a fault in the cochlea or in the auditory nerve. If the fault is in the organ of Corti, a hearing aid can sometimes help, but if there is nerve damage, hearing loss is normally permanent. People born deaf usually suffer from this condition.

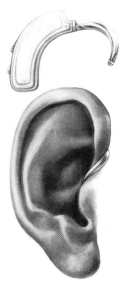

The modern hearing aid is a tiny electronic amplifier which fits behind or even inside the ear. It increases the volume of sound entering the ear, and can relieve some forms of partial deafness.

Experiencing sound

The grooves in a phonograph record reproduce sound waves very closely. Movement of the stylus, following the grooves very closely, is transformed into electrical impulses which are amplified to produce sounds.

Some of the techniques used to teach deaf people can also help a person with normal hearing understand how sound works.

A tuning fork is normally used to check the tuning of musical instruments. It is a two-pronged metal fork which produces an exact musical note when struck so that the prongs vibrate. Each vibration of the prongs produces a wave and the number of movements or vibrations each second is the frequency of the sound (in cycles per second, or hertz).

Touch the vibrating prongs very gently, and you will feel the movements. Touch the handle end against your head near the temple where the skin is thin, and you will "hear" the sound very loudly, but not through your ears. The tuning fork is passing vibrations directly through the bones of the skull to the cochlea. A deaf person with a damaged middle ear can still "hear" sounds transmitted in this way. Some modern stereo earphones play music directly into the inner ear using this principle of bone conduction.

A person born deaf does not know at first how to produce a sound. And once sounds have been produced, it is very difficult to control them enough to talk properly if you cannot hear your own voice.

Deaf children are taught to understand sound by means of a balloon held between the face of the child and that of the teacher. As the teacher speaks, the child can feel the vibration of the balloon through the skin. The child attempts to make a sound which produces the same vibration, and in this way begins to learn control over his or her voice.

A totally deaf child can understand sound by feeling the vibration caused when a drum is struck, or by touching a vibrating turning fork.

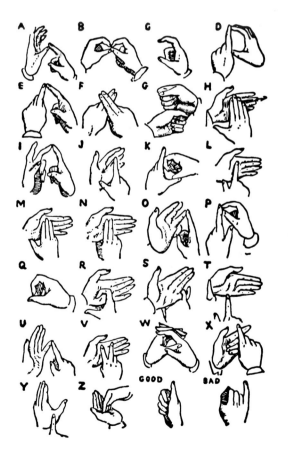

This is one version of a sign language. Today most deaf children are taught to speak using techniques which allow them to feel the sound waves produced in the throat.

The sense of balance

Our sense of balance, or equilibrium, is a very important function of the ear. Two quite different senses are involved in keeping our equilibrium. These measure the movement of the head, and measure gravity, which tells us where the head is positioned in relation to "up" and "down."

The organs which measure these two conditions are called the **vestibular apparatus**. This is an outgrowth from the membranous labyrinth (the other part is the cochlea).

Movement is detected by a system of three curved, liquid-filled tubes, the semicircular canals. The liquid they contain is endolymph, like that in the cochlear duct running through the middle of the cochlea. The tubes are shaped like arches, anchored at each end to the bulge of the utricle. Their position is very important to understanding how they work. One tube is horizontal, while the others stand vertically in the ear, with their arches pointing away from each other at 90 degrees. Their arrangement is like the three sides at the corner of a box.

In a spirit level, position is indicated by an air bubble in a tube filled with liquid.
The inner ear is also liquid filled, but it detects changes in position by movement of the liquid.

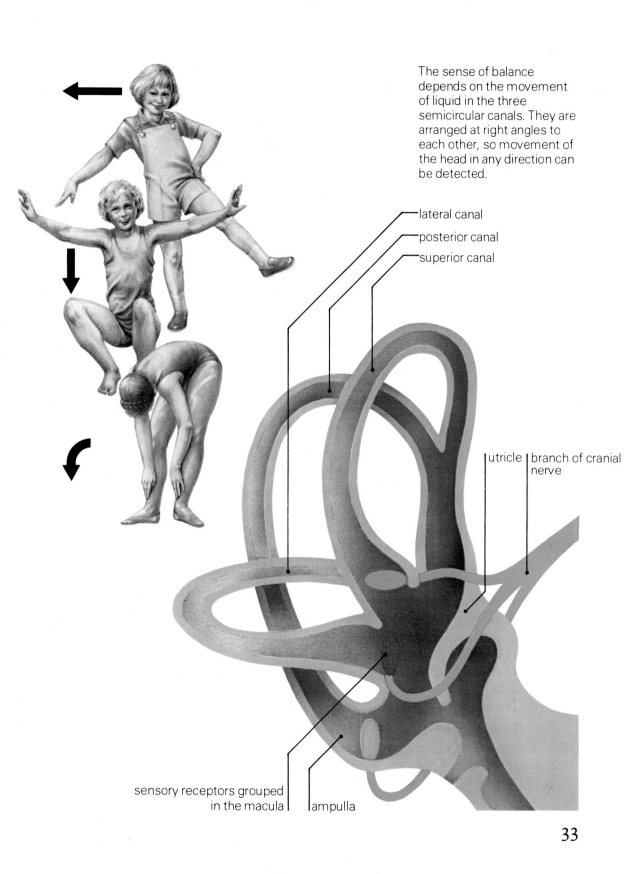

The sense of balance depends on the movement of liquid in the three semicircular canals. They are arranged at right angles to each other, so movement of the head in any direction can be detected.

lateral canal

posterior canal

superior canal

utricle | branch of cranial nerve

sensory receptors grouped in the macula | ampulla

33

Measuring movement

Our sense of movement of the head depends on the liquid filling of the semicircular canals. Look at a cup of coffee, and twist the cup sharply. As the cup rotates, the coffee stays where it is. This is exactly what happens in the semicircular canals. Depending on which way the head turns, the semicircular canals rotate with the head, while the endolymph within tries to remain in the same place, due to a phenomenon called inertia. This relative movement of the canal and its liquid contents stimulates special receptor cells to provide the sensation of movement.

In each ampulla is a group of nerve cells, each carrying a long sensory hair. They are called the **crista**. Over the cells, and surrounding the hairs, is a mass of soft material like gelatine, the **cupola**. This almost blocks the duct through the ampulla, but it is free to move from side to side.

As the head turns, it moves the semi-circular canals with it, but the endolymph tends to lag behind the movement. The different rate of movement causes the cupola to be bent to one side, allowing endolymph to flow along the canal. This in turn bends the sensory hairs, causing the cells to produce signals which are passed to the brain. The faster the head moves, the more signals will

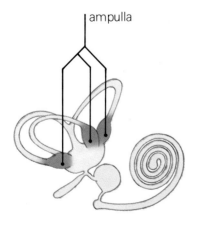
ampulla

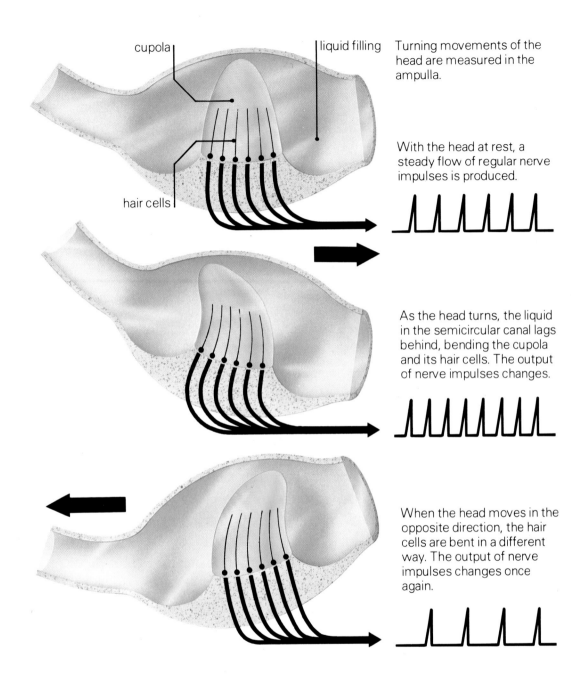

cupola

liquid filling

hair cells

Turning movements of the head are measured in the ampulla.

With the head at rest, a steady flow of regular nerve impulses is produced.

As the head turns, the liquid in the semicircular canal lags behind, bending the cupola and its hair cells. The output of nerve impulses changes.

When the head moves in the opposite direction, the hair cells are bent in a different way. The output of nerve impulses changes once again.

be produced, so the brain will know how fast the head is turning. Depending on which canals produce signals, the brain will also know whether the head is moving up, down or sideways.

Which way is up?

Sea-sickness or any other form of motion-sickness is caused when continuous movement causes the liquid inside the organs of balance to swirl about. At the same time, stony otoliths in the macula give false readings to the sense organs.

The semicircular canals measure turning movements of the head. Movements in a straight line, together with the actual position of the head, are measured by other parts of the vestibular apparatus. The saccule and the utricle both contain special sensory areas called **macula**. They are positioned at right angles, so that when one macula is horizontal, the other is at right angles to it.

In each macula are banks of sensory cells, each carrying a large hair. As with other sensory cells in the ear, bending the hair causes the cell to produce a signal. A jelly-like layer covers the macula, and embedded in this are chalky granules, called **otoliths**.

Like the liquid in the semicircular canals, otoliths have inertia, tending to remain still as the head moves. As the head shifts, the otoliths try to remain in their original position in the jelly, causing the sensory hairs to bend and generate signals.

The sensory cells in the macula are arranged in patterns which allow the brain to decide in which direction the movement has been made. The brain is also informed as to which direction gravity is pulling, by its effect on the otoliths.

Measurement of gravity can be confused when driving fast over a humped bridge, and

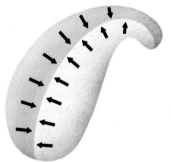

utricle ——
macula ——

—— saccule
—— macula

the otoliths "float" for a moment. Astronauts experience more pronounced effects, without any gravity to stabilize the movements of the otoliths.

Signals from the semicircular canals, utricle and saccule are all carried to the base of the brain by the auditory nerve. From here, instructions are relayed to the muscles of the legs, back and neck so tiny muscular adjustments can be made automatically to keep us standing or moving steadily. We are not aware of these **reflex** activities, but a few signals reach the conscious part of the brain, so we are aware of our position and movements.

Hair cells in the macula are arranged so that the exact direction and amount of movement is detected.

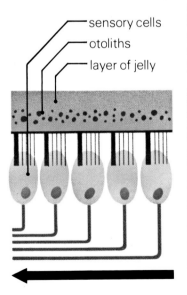

sensory cells
otoliths
layer of jelly

Movement in a straight line causes the sensory hairs to be stimulated due to movement of stony otoliths, embedded in a coating of jelly.

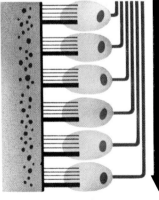

direction of movement

Glossary

Amplitude: the height of a sound wave; associated with the loudness of a sound.

Ampulla: swelling at the base of each semicircular canal, containing sensory cells which detect movement of the fluid within the canals.

Auditory nerve: the nerve carrying electrical signals from the inner ear to the base of the brain.

Auricle: outer flap of the ear. Also called the pinna.

Basilar membrane: thin sheet of material in the cochlea which vibrates in response to movements in the liquid filling the cochlea. Part of the organ of Corti.

Bony labyrinth: Cavity in each side of the skull which contains the inner-ear mechanism. It closely follows the shape of the cochlea and the semicircular canals.

Cerumen: ear wax, produced in the ear canal to lubricate and protect its delicate lining.

Cochlea: coiled tubular structure in which vibrations caused by sound waves are converted into nerve impulses.

Cortex: surface of the brain, on which information received from the ears and other sense organs is processed.

Crista: patches of sensory cells within the ampullae of the semicircular canals. They detect fluid movement.

Cupola: mass of jelly covering the sensory hairs in the ampullae of the semicircular canals. The jelly shifts as the surrounding fluid moves, bending the hairs and generating a nerve impulse, which is then passed on to the brain.

Decibel: the most common unit used to measure the loudness of a sound.

Ear canal: the short tube conducting sound from the outer ear to the eardrum or tympanic membrane.

Eardrum: thin membrane stretched across the inner opening of the ear canal. Its vibrations are passed to the bones of the inner ear. Also called the tympanic membrane.

Endolymph: liquid filling the central duct of the cochlea. It surrounds the organ of Corti.

Eustachian tube: connects the middle ear with the throat at the back of the mouth. Used to equalize pressure with the atmosphere, protecting the delicate eardrum.

Frequency: the number of vibrations per second of any sound. Frequency controls how deep, or shrill, the sound seems.

Incus: central bone of the three small bones in the middle ear. Takes part in carrying sound from the eardrum to the cochlea. Also called the anvil.

Inner ear: complicated structure inside a cavity in the skull, which contains the sensory organs for hearing, balance and position.

Macula: area containing sensory cells, within the organs of balance, which measure head position.

Malleus: tiny bone attached to the eardrum, which passes sound vibrations on to the incus. Also called the hammer.

Membranous labyrinth: structure of the inner ear, comprising the cochlea and semicircular canals, extending from the bulky saccule and utricle.

Middle ear: air-filled cavity in the skull, containing the malleus, incus and stapes bones. It transfers and amplifies sound received by the eardrum.

Organ of Corti: strip of sensory cells resting on the basilar membrane in the cochlea. It receives vibrations in the endolymph, converting them to nerve impulses.

Ossicles: the bones of the middle ear: malleus, incus and stapes.

Otoliths: stony particles in the macula of the inner ear, which help in our awareness of gravity and movement.

Outer ear: the external part of the ear (the pinna), the ear canal and the eardrum.

Perilymph: watery liquid filling the outer pair of tubes running through the cochlea.

Pinna: the outer, visible part of the ear. Also called the auricle.

Reflex: automatic response of the body, such as is used in maintaining our balance.

Saccule: area of the inner ear where some of the organs measuring position and gravity are positioned.

Semicircular canals: fluid-filled curved tubes, part of the membranous labyrinth. Movement of fluid through the canals makes us aware of turning sensations as the head is moved.

Sound wave: areas of alternating low and high pressure, which move through air (or any other substance) and, when collected in the ear, are interpreted as sound.

Stapes: one of the three ossicles which passes vibrations into the cochlea through the oval window. Also called the stirrup.

Tectorial membrane: long, thin strip of membrane in contact with sensory hairs in the organ of Corti. Sound vibrations move the tectorial membrane and the sensory cells relative to each other, producing nerve impulses.

Tympanic membrane: the eardrum.

Utricle: with the saccule, comprises the areas in which gravity and position are sensed.

Vestibular apparatus: areas at the larger end of the cochlea, where organs measuring movement, gravity and position are situated.

Wave length: distance between the peaks of successive sound waves.

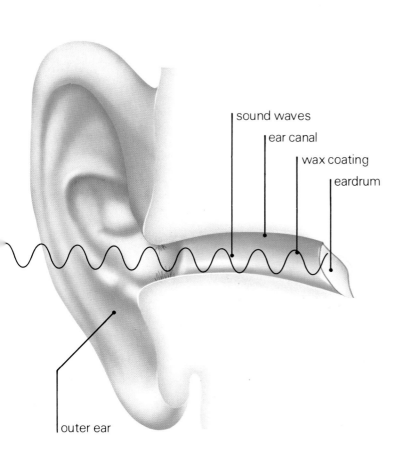

sound waves

ear canal

wax coating

eardrum

outer ear

Index

Printed in Great Britain by Cambus Litho, East Kilbride, Scotland